TinkerActive WORKBOOKS

SECOND GRADE · SCIENCE · AGES 7–8

by Megan Hewes Butler

illustrated by Tae Won Yu

educational consulting by Lindsay Frevert

Odd Dot · New York

Properties of Matter

All things are made up of matter. All the objects around you, like a chair, a tree, or a pet, are matter. Matter can be described by how it looks, feels, and more!

Circle one word to describe each piece of matter.

Hardness

| hard | soft |

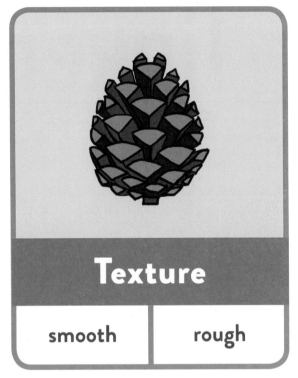

Texture

| smooth | rough |

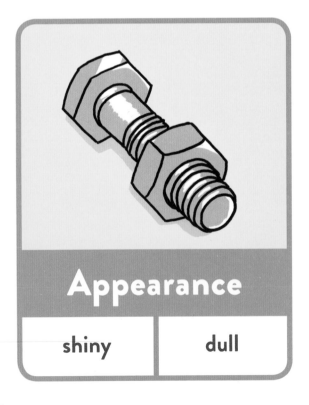

Appearance

| shiny | dull |

Flexibility

| flexible | stiff |

Observe your pencil. Then answer each question.

What color is it?

_____

_____

_____

What shape is it?

_____

_____

_____

What does it feel like?

_____

_____

_____

What does it sound like when you tap it?

_____

_____

_____

Matter has different properties—for example, paper is thin, while a tree trunk is thick. Because of these differences, different types of matter are useful for different needs.

Read the text aloud. Then circle the object that each MotMot needs and explain why you chose that object.

Enid needs a flexible material to wrap her trophy in.

 **or**

Why? _____

_____

Frank needs a strong material to make a leash for his pet alligator.

 **or**

Why? _____

_____

Brian needs a soft material to clean this mirror with.

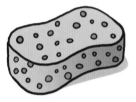 **or**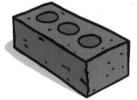

Why? _____

_____

Dimitri needs a heavy material to hold open this door.

 **or**

Why? _____

_____

Hunt for matter around you. Find an object that fits each description below. Then write its name or draw it.

A material that is
WARM

A material that is
STICKY

A material that is
RED

A material that is
WET

A material that is
BUMPY

A material that is
SOFT

A material that is
BENDABLE

Choose something of your own to observe, and draw it. Then circle all the descriptions that apply, or fill in your own.

My object is a _____.

COLOR

Other: _____

SHAPE

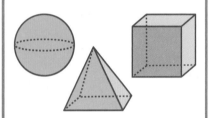

Other: _____

TEXTURE

- Smooth

- Bumpy

- Hairy

Other: _____

SIZE

- Small

- Medium

- Large

FLEXIBILITY

- Flexible

- Rigid

- Mixed

HARDNESS

- Soft

- Hard

- Mixed

I notice that my object is also _____

_____

_____.

LET'S START! GATHER THESE TOOLS AND MATERIALS.

Markers

Paper

2 or more cans

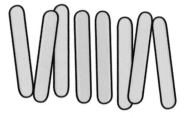
10 or more craft sticks

10 or more plastic cups

Aluminum foil

LET'S TINKER!

Observe each of your materials.

- What color is it?
- Is it round?
- Pointed?
- Slippery?

Describe them all.

- How are they the same?
- How are they different?

Group materials that have something in common.

LET'S MAKE: TOWERING TOWER

Make a tall tower with your materials.

Ask yourself: What qualities should the materials have in order to make a tall tower?

Choose rigid and strong materials that can be stacked without bending. **Choose** wide materials that can't fall over. How can you stack the materials to make the tower taller and stronger?

LET'S ENGINEER!

Enid and Callie are playing hide-and-seek with the other MotMots. Enid wants to send a message to Callie, who is hiding behind the pantry door.

How can Enid send Callie a message?

Think about what shape of material can be passed under a door.

- What other properties should the material have?
- How can the materials be combined to solve the problem?

Write your own secret message. You can **add** stickers from page 129.

Test your ideas by trying to send a note under a door.

PROJECT 1: DONE!
Get your sticker!

Assemble and Disassemble Parts

Many objects around you are made up of multiple parts. Look at the swing and study its parts. Next,

- Cross out the chains.
- Underline the seat.
- Circle the hangers.

Which parts are left over? _____

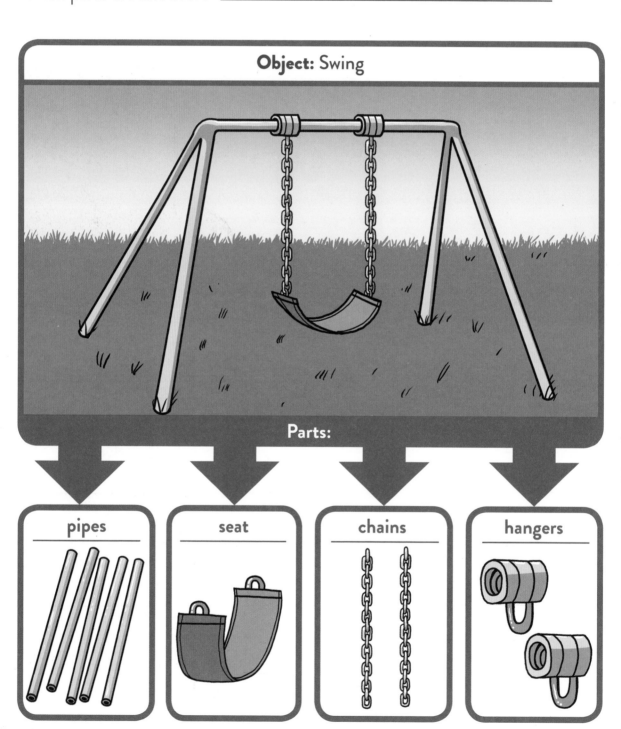

Object: Swing

Parts:

| pipes | seat | chains | hangers |

Write the names of and draw the parts that make up this object.

Object: Tire Swing

Parts:

Find one object around you that is made up of multiple parts. Then write about the object and its parts.

_____

_____

_____

Many objects can be broken into parts. Then the parts can be used to build something new.

Read the story aloud. Then follow the instructions.

The MotMots love to pick juicy apples to eat. Every time they want an apple, they walk over a wooden bridge to climb the apple tree. It's a long walk, but the apples are so yummy!

Write the names of and draw the parts that make up the bridge.

Parts of the bridge:

buckets

Enid loves apples the most. If she rides her bike,
she can get to the apple tree more quickly and pick
apples more often. She rides to the park, but she
can't get her bike over the bridge.

What could Enid build with the same parts so she could ride her bike over
the stream? Draw it.

Callie and her friends are camping. They want to picnic, but it looks like it will rain soon. How can Callie keep her friends and the food dry?

Look at the materials and parts that Callie has at the campsite.

butterfly net

sleeping bag

picnic basket

leaves

jump rope

rocks

sticks

picnic blanket

Describe how Callie can solve the problem.

_____

_____

_____

Draw what she can build to solve the problem.

LET'S START!

Tape

Paper

Markers

Aluminum foil

4–6 toothpicks

4–6 cotton balls

4–6 rubber bands

1 or more toilet paper rolls

Beans, nuts, or dried pasta

LET'S TINKER!

Put your materials together so they make a new object or do something new. **Stack** them, fit one inside another, or attach them.

What new object did you make?

What can it do?

LET'S MAKE: ROBOT PARTS

Make a robot. **Choose** parts for the body, legs, and other features—like a head, arms, antennae, and buttons. You can **add** stickers from page 129. How can you make the parts stay together?

LET'S ENGINEER!

Amelia wants to play music with her friends. But there are no instruments left!

How can Amelia make music with her friends?

Combine your materials to make an instrument.

- How can the materials be combined to make sound?
- Is your instrument quiet or loud?
- What kind of sound does it make?

PROJECT 2: DONE!
Get your sticker!

States of Matter

Matter can exist in different forms, including a solid, a liquid, or a gas.

| A **solid** has shape and volume. | A **liquid** has volume, but no shape. It flows. | A **gas** has no volume or shape. It fills the volume of its container. |

Read about the matter. Then draw what you predict will happen when these cups are emptied.

A grape is a solid, so each one has a shape.

Grape juice is a liquid, so it has no shape.

Brian is searching for solids, liquids, and gases. Fill in the state of matter of each object.

Solids, liquids, and gases have different properties, and each can be used for different purposes.

Read what each MotMot needs aloud. Then circle the material that will solve each problem, and fill in whether it is a solid, a liquid, or a gas.

Dimitri needs something to drink.

Callie needs something firm to stay between two cookies.

He needs a _____.

She needs a _____.

Frank needs something that can expand to fill this balloon.

Enid needs something she can pour into this vase.

HELIUM GAS

SODA

He needs a _____.

She needs a _____.

The molecules that make up a solid, a liquid, and a gas act differently.

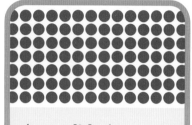

In a **solid**, the molecules are tightly packed. They jiggle only a little.

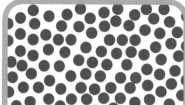

In a **liquid**, the molecules are close together but have some room to move and slide around.

In a **gas**, the molecules have lots of space to move around quickly and freely!

Join the MotMots and move your body like a molecule! Then draw yourself dancing in each state: solid, liquid, and gas.

Jiggle your body a little like a **solid**.

Move and slide your body around like a **liquid**.

Stretch your body to move freely and quickly like a **gas**.

Matter is in different states all around you. Hunt for examples in your home and follow the directions below.

Describe and draw a **solid**.

_____

_____

_____

Describe and draw a **liquid**.

_____

_____

_____

Can you see a **gas** in your home? If so, describe and draw it. If not, why do you think you can't see any gases?

_____

_____

_____

_____

LET'S START!

GATHER THESE TOOLS AND MATERIALS.

Aluminum foil

Plastic wrap

1 or more
plastic cups

4–6
rubber bands

4–6
drinking straws

Water

Toys

Measuring cup

5–8 spoonfuls
of cornstarch

Small backpack
or bag

LET'S TINKER!

Solids have their own shape—they do not need a container to hold them. **Change** the shapes of the foil, plastic wrap, cup, rubber bands, or straws. **Fold**, tear, bend, and twist the materials.

Liquids cannot hold their own shape—they need a container. **Make** something that can hold a liquid and fill it with water.

Air is a gas that is all around us, but we cannot see it. **Make** bubbles of air that you can see! **Fill** a cup halfway with water. **Lower** your straw to the bottom of the cup and blow softly. What do you see?

LET'S MAKE: PLAY GOOP!

1. Measure $\frac{1}{4}$ cup of water into your bowl.

2. Stir in 5 to 8 heaping spoonfuls of cornstarch, one at a time. The goop is ready when you can still stir it, even though it is hard to do so.

3. Play!

- Does it feel like a liquid or a solid?
- Does it move like a liquid or a solid?
- Can you make a ball—a solid—with it?
- In what ways does the goop act like a liquid?
- In what ways does it act like a solid?

Caution: When you are done experimenting, do not wash the goop down a sink drain. Instead, throw it in the trash.

LET'S ENGINEER!

Frank is packing for a trip. He needs to fit all his things into his sack, but it is filling up fast. Each item is a solid and takes up space.

How can Frank fit all his things into his sack?

Try to fit all your materials in your bag, as if you are going on a trip. How can you make the materials take up less space? Can any of them change shape?

PROJECT 3: DONE!
Get your sticker!

Temperature

Temperature is a measure of how much heat is in an object. Heating up an object or cooling it down can cause changes that we can see.

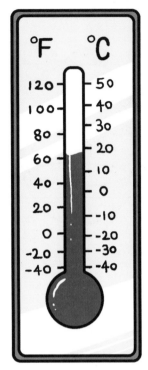

When ice cream heats up enough, it changes from a solid to a liquid.

Write about and draw what happens when an ice-cream cone is in the hot sun.

_____

_____

_____

When water cools down enough, it changes from a liquid to a solid.

Write about and draw what happens when a pond full of water is in freezing cold weather.

_____

_____

_____

Some changes that happen from heating and cooling are reversible. This means that the matter can change back to the way it was.

Some changes that happen from heating and cooling are *not* reversible. This means that the matter *cannot* go back to the way it was.

Observe each change below. Then write a ✔ next to the sentence that accurately describes the temperature changes.

☐ The water freezes and becomes ice. Then the ice thaws and becomes water.

☐ The water freezes and becomes ice. The ice cannot become water again.

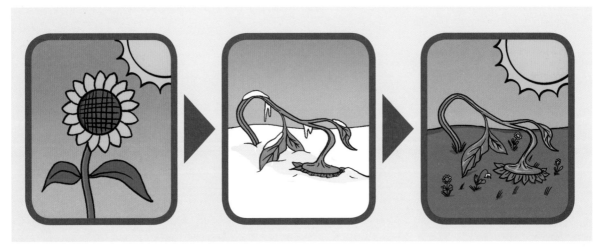

☐ The flower freezes and dies. The flower is alive again when it gets warm.

☐ The flower freezes and dies. The flower cannot come back to life when it gets warm again.

Look at each object as it heats up and cools down. Then write a ✔ next to "reversible" or "not reversible."

This change is:

☐ reversible   ☐ not reversible

This change is:

☐ reversible   ☐ not reversible

This change is:

☐ reversible   ☐ not reversible

Hunt for objects around you that are affected by temperature. Draw what you find. Then answer each question.

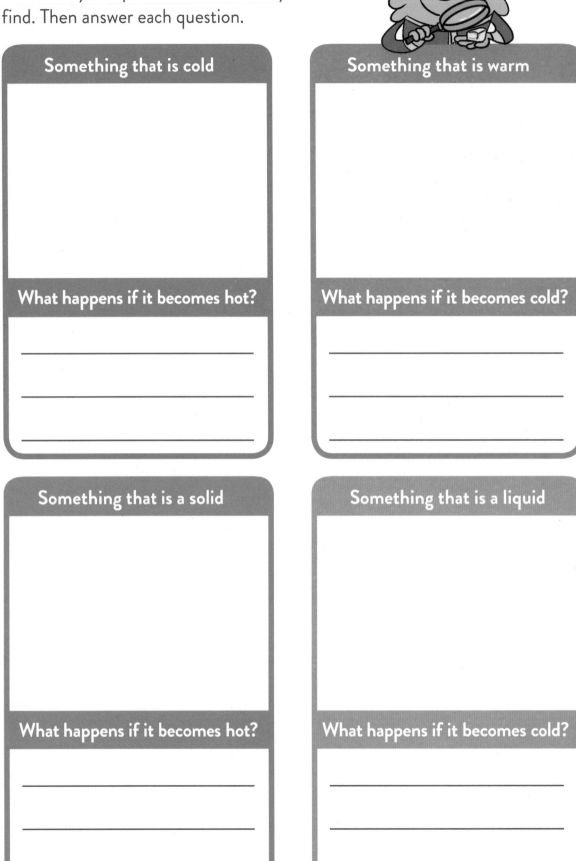

Something that is cold

What happens if it becomes hot?

_____

_____

_____

Something that is warm

What happens if it becomes cold?

_____

_____

_____

Something that is a solid

What happens if it becomes hot?

_____

_____

_____

Something that is a liquid

What happens if it becomes cold?

_____

_____

_____

Find food in your kitchen that changes when you cook it. Then draw or write to answer each question.

What does it look like before it is cooked?	What does it look like after it is cooked?

The change is:

☐ reversible   ☐ not reversible

Find something in your freezer that you can thaw. Then draw or write to answer each question.

What does it look like before it is thawed?	As it warms up, what changes do you observe?

The change is:

☐ reversible   ☐ not reversible

LET'S START! GATHER THESE TOOLS AND MATERIALS.

Ice cubes

Leaf

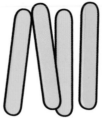
Craft sticks

Crayons

Cup of water

Piece of string
2–3 feet long

Aluminum foil

Modeling Clay

LET'S TINKER!

Change the temperature of your materials by blowing on them.

- Which materials change?
- Are the changes reversible or not reversible?

LET'S MAKE: FREEZER EXPERIMENT

1. **Observe** your materials.

- What do they feel like? Look like? Smell like?
- Do they bend or break when you touch them?

2. Put the materials in the freezer. **Predict** what will happen to them.

3. Take the materials out of the freezer in a few hours and make new observations.

- How did they change?
- Do any of them look different? Feel different? Smell different?
- Were your predictions correct?

Temperature

LET'S ENGINEER!

Callie wants an ice-cold drink, so she breaks off some icicles for her juice. But when she holds the cold icicles in her warm hands, they start to melt!

How can she carry the icicles to her kitchen without melting them?

Design a container that can keep ice colder than your hands do. How can you keep the ice cubes away from the warmth of your hands? **Use** ice cubes to test which materials can keep ice frozen.

PROJECT 4: DONE!
Get your sticker!

Water Cycle

Over 70% of Earth's surface is covered in water. Water is the only thing that can naturally be found on Earth as a solid, a liquid, and a gas.

Write a ✔ next to the correct form of water.

☐ Solid
☐ Liquid

☐ Solid
☐ Liquid

☐ Solid
☐ Liquid

☐ Solid
☐ Liquid

☐ Solid
☐ Liquid

☐ Solid
☐ Liquid

Animals live on and in the water—both solid and liquid—all over Earth. Draw a line to connect each animal to its water habitat.

sailfish

dolphin

emperor penguin

stingray

polar bear

POLAR HABITAT

OPEN OCEAN HABITAT

The water cycle describes the way water moves to and from the land, sky, and ocean. Water that starts on the land becomes a gas in the sky, and then becomes a solid or liquid that falls back to Earth. The water cycle repeats over and over again.

Look at the water cycle, and read the descriptions aloud. Then answer each question.

Evaporation

Water from rivers, lakes, streams, and oceans changes to water vapor when the Sun heats Earth.

Condensation

Water vapor in the air changes into small drops of liquid water when it gets colder. The small water drops come together to make clouds.

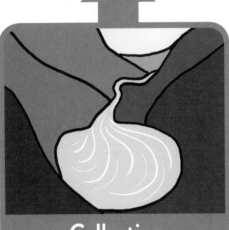

Collection

Liquid water collects in rivers, lakes, streams, and oceans.

Precipitation

Water falls to Earth from clouds as rain, hail, or snow.

You breathe on a cold day and you can see your breath.

Is this water vapor a **liquid** or a **gas**?

_____

Clouds become heavy with water and raindrops fall to Earth.

Are these drops **precipitation** or **evaporation**?

_____

You leave a bucket of water outside for a few days, and later you find less water in the bucket.

Is the water **evaporating** or **precipitating**?

_____

You add ice to a glass of water, and water drops form on the outside as it cools.

Are these drops **condensation** or **evaporation**?

_____

Which parts of the water cycle have you seen for yourself?

_____

All forms of water can be seen in the weather. Observe and record your weather for a week.

	Draw the weather outside your home.	Is there any precipitation?	Is it a solid, liquid, or gas?
Sunday		☐ yes ☐ no	_____
Monday		☐ yes ☐ no	_____
Tuesday		☐ yes ☐ no	_____
Wednesday		☐ yes ☐ no	_____
Thursday		☐ yes ☐ no	_____
Friday		☐ yes ☐ no	_____
Saturday		☐ yes ☐ no	_____

Severe weather events often have precipitation. Read each definition. Then draw a line to the matching picture.

In a **hailstorm**, balls and lumps of ice, called hail, fall like rain.

In a **thunderstorm**, heavy rain falls. There is thunder, lightning, and sometimes wind or hail.

A **hurricane** is a storm that forms over the ocean. Fast-spinning winds pick up water, move at over 74 miles per hour, and make heavy rain.

A **blizzard** is a cold-weather storm with strong winds. Snow is blown so quickly that seeing is difficult.

LET'S START! GATHER THESE TOOLS AND MATERIALS.

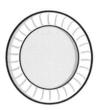
Paper plate

Permanent markers

2 or more plastic sandwich bags

Water

Tape

Water bottle

Ice cubes

Aluminum foil

LET'S TINKER!

Place some of your materials in the bowl of water. **Watch** what happens when they get wet.

- How do they change?
- Do any of them stay the same?
- How do they move in the water?
- What else do you notice?

LET'S MAKE: YOUR OWN WATER CYCLE

1. Using the permanent markers, **draw** an ocean at the bottom of a plastic bag and clouds at the top.

2. Fill your bag with about 1 inch of water and seal the top tightly.

3. Tape the bag to a window with lots of sunlight.

5

Water
Cycle

4. Watch the water inside your bag "cycle" over several days! Can you tell when the water evaporates, condenses, and precipitates?

LET'S ENGINEER!

Dimitri wants to put ice cubes in his water bottle, but the ice cubes he has won't fit through the neck of the bottle.

How can he freeze more water so the cubes fit into the bottle?

Design a new ice cube shape that can fit into the bottle. What shapes can solve the problem?

Make a mold with your foil, pour in water, and put it in your freezer. After a few hours, **remove** your new ice cube. Does it fit into a water bottle?

PROJECT 5: DONE!
Get your sticker!

Earth's Surface

Earth's surface is made of rocks and dirt, and it is constantly changing. Many things cause these changes, including animals, plants, people, and the weather.

Look at each each picture. Then write a ✔ next to what caused the change to Earth's surface.

☐ Animals ☐ People
☐ Plants ☐ Weather

☐ Animals ☐ People
☐ Plants ☐ Weather

☐ Animals ☐ People
☐ Plants ☐ Weather

☐ Animals ☐ People
☐ Plants ☐ Weather

☐ Animals   ☐ People
☐ Plants   ☐ Weather

☐ Animals   ☐ People
☐ Plants   ☐ Weather

☐ Animals   ☐ People
☐ Plants   ☐ Weather

☐ Animals   ☐ People
☐ Plants   ☐ Weather

Some effects of wind and water on Earth's surface can be slowed down or even stopped.

Read each definition aloud. Then draw a line to the matching picture.

A **windbreak** is a row of trees or other plants used to protect the ground from erosion by the wind.

A **dam** is a barrier built in a river to hold back or slow down the water. Dams also release water when needed.

A **levee** is a large wall or mound of earth that provides protection from high water and storms. A levee does not move.

When it rains, the river in Tinker Town usually overflows. The water floods onto the playground where the MotMots play. They can't play there until the water is absorbed by the ground and the ground dries again.

What could stop the flooding? Draw your solution.

Describe your solution.

_____

_____

_____

_____

Circle the MotMot in each pair of pictures who is doing something to protect Earth's surface.

Write about and draw what you can do at school to help protect Earth's surface.

_____

_____

Write about and draw what you can do at home to help protect Earth's surface.

_____

_____

LET'S START!

GATHER THESE TOOLS AND MATERIALS.

4 or more craft sticks

5 or more rocks

5 or more buttons

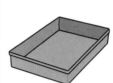
Large metal tray or pan

Dirt, mud, or modeling clay

Sticks

3 or more leaves

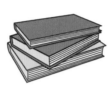
Stack of books

Large paper cup

Water

LET'S TINKER!

One way that animals change the surface of Earth is by making prints and impressions on the dirt.

Make your own fingerprints or handprints. **Find** materials you can use to make the prints in.

- Which materials do not work for making prints? Why?

- What other kinds of prints can you make?

1. Lay 4 craft sticks in a grid.

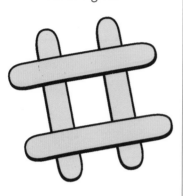

2. Get 5 rocks for yourself and 5 buttons for the other player.

3. Play tic-tac-toe!

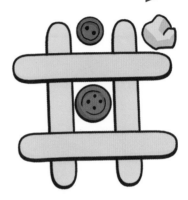

LET'S ENGINEER!

Enid wants to put a bench in a sunny spot so she can sit and read outside. But the only sunny spot is exactly where a stream runs.

How can Enid change the path of the stream using natural materials?

Make a model to find out how to change the path of a stream. **Work** outdoors, or work indoors using a sink or a bathtub.

- Place a smooth layer of natural materials in the bottom of the tray. Try using mud, dirt, rocks, sticks, and leaves, or use modeling clay.

- Then tilt the tray and put a stack of books under one side to keep it slanted.

- Using a cup, pour a little bit of water at the top of your tray. Watch where the water goes.

- Use the natural materials in the tray to build a dam, walls, barriers, and hills to change the path of the water. Pour water in again and observe what happens.

PROJECT 6: DONE!
Get your sticker!

Changes on Earth

Some changes on Earth's surface happen slowly, and other changes happen quickly. For example, most volcanoes erupt quickly. But each volcano is unique. Some volcanoes take weeks or even years to finish erupting.

Read the stages of a volcanic eruption. Then write the numbers 1, 2, and 3 to put the eruption in order.

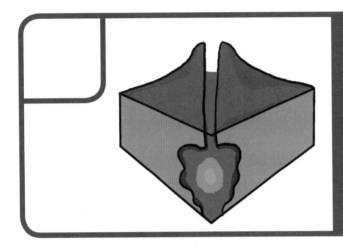

When a volcano becomes active, magma gathers beneath the volcano. Sometimes Earth shakes, like an earthquake, as the volcano begins to erupt.

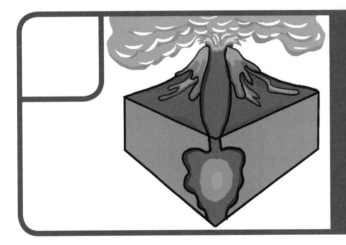

An explosion of gases pushes the magma out of the volcano. Once it is on Earth's surface, we call it lava. Lava oozes down the slopes, and ash fills the sky.

The lava finishes erupting. The empty volcano is weak and often collapses into the magma chamber, leaving a crater.

Read about each way Earth changes quickly. Then follow the directions.

An earthquake is when the ground shakes because Earth's crust moves deep inside it.

Draw how this place might look just after an **earthquake**.

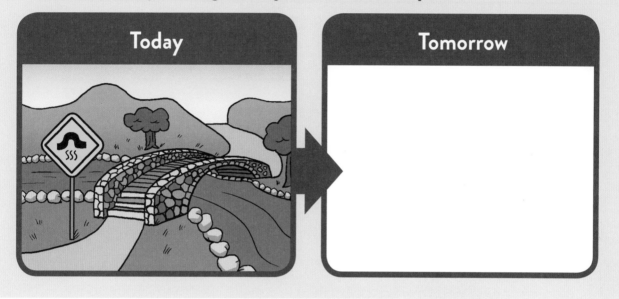

A landslide is when rocks, mud, or other parts of Earth's surface slide down a mountain or hill.

Draw how this place might look just after a **landslide**.

Some changes on Earth happen slowly—so slowly that no one can observe them.

Read the report aloud.

All About Erosion

Erosion is when Earth's surface is slowly worn away. Over time, the shape of the land changes.

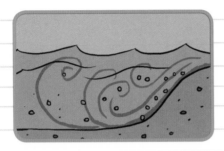 

Water causes most erosion. Bits of sand and small rocks are picked up by a river and moved. The Grand Canyon, in Arizona, is an example of water erosion over a very long time.

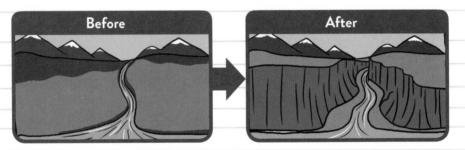

Ice and **wind** can cause erosion, too. Glaciers are made of flowing ice. They pick up sand and rocks as they move along, just like a river does. Wind can also hit a rock and carry tiny pieces of it away, changing the rock's shape!

Erosion happens all around us, but it happens so slowly that it is difficult to see. Erosion happens a little bit at a time, but over many years it can make big changes to Earth.

Draw how erosion might make this place look next year and in one hundred years.

Today

Tomorrow

Next Year

100 Years

Do these events change Earth slowly or quickly? Write a ✔ next to the correct speed.

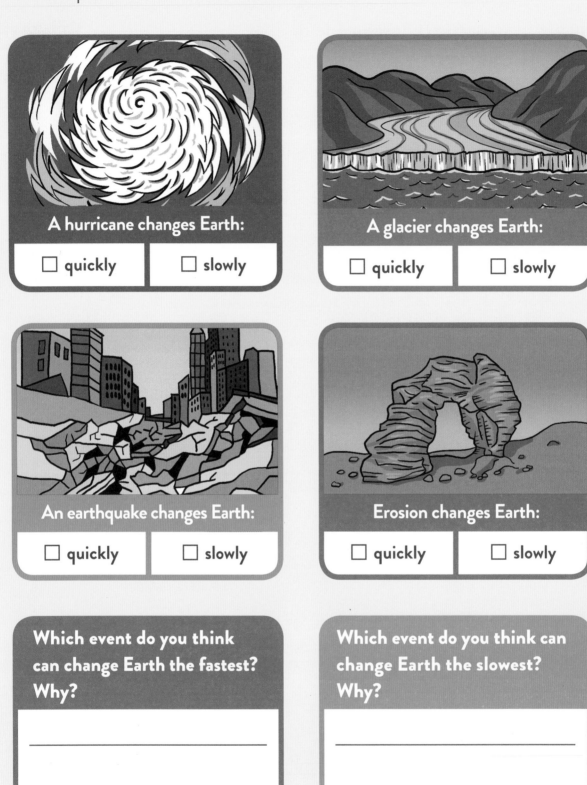

A hurricane changes Earth:

☐ quickly   ☐ slowly

A glacier changes Earth:

☐ quickly   ☐ slowly

An earthquake changes Earth:

☐ quickly   ☐ slowly

Erosion changes Earth:

☐ quickly   ☐ slowly

Which event do you think can change Earth the fastest? Why?

_____

_____

_____

_____

Which event do you think can change Earth the slowest? Why?

_____

_____

_____

_____

Draw how Earth's surface around you changes.

Are the changes you see fast or slow? Write about what you observe.

_____

_____

_____

_____

LET'S START! GATHER THESE TOOLS AND MATERIALS.

4–6 cotton balls

4–6 pieces of dried pasta

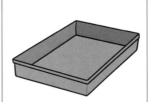
Aluminum foil

4–6 paper clips

Tall plastic or glass cup

Baking soda

Dish soap

Large metal pan

Vinegar

LET'S TINKER!

Which of the following materials can be changed: cotton balls, dried pasta, aluminum foil, and paper clips? **Make** them change if you can. **Bend** them, crush them, wet them, scratch them, expand them, or try something else.

- Do the materials change slowly or quickly?

- Are there any materials that you can't change? Why?

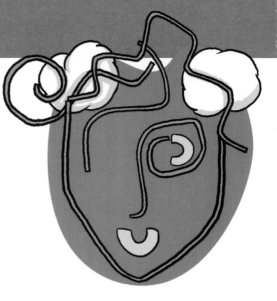

LET'S MAKE: A VOLCANIC ERUPTION

1. **Pour** 2 spoonfuls of baking soda and a squirt of dish soap into a cup.

2. **Place** the cup on a tray or pan, and use the other materials to build a model volcano around the cup.

3. Dump about a cup of vinegar into the container.

4. Watch the "lava" flow!

LET'S ENGINEER!

Brian's little brother loves building sandcastles at the playground. But every time they return to the playground, the sandcastle is gone. And every time, Brian's little brother doesn't understand why and cries. Brian wants to teach his brother about the way weathering breaks rocks into smaller bits, and then erosion slowly moves the smaller rock pieces over time.

How can Brian show his little brother weathering and erosion?

Choose some materials that can be broken into smaller pieces. **Break** them apart. **Ask** yourself: How can I create wind to blow the pieces away? **Describe** the process of weathering and erosion aloud as you show it to a friend or family member.

PROJECT 7: DONE!
Get your sticker!

Maps

Maps show where things are located. Some maps show where land and water features are, while other maps show roads and where people live. Maps can be big or small, flat, round, or even digital—like on a computer or phone.

Draw a line from each map name to the matching map in Enid's home.

a globe

a trail map

a weather map

a train map

a star map

What kinds of maps do you and your family use?

_____

_____

Physical maps show the geography of an area. This includes the shape of the land, types of land, and bodies of water.

The MotMots are meeting friends for a picnic. Read the directions aloud. Then draw their path on the map. Use the landforms and bodies of water as your guides.

cape

cliff

bay

delta

- Move three spaces and turn right at the cliff.
- Move two steps and turn left.
- Move seven spaces toward the river.
- Turn left and move two spaces.
- Turn right and move four steps toward the marsh.
- Turn right and move seven steps toward the lake.
- Turn right, move two steps, and stop to have a picnic!

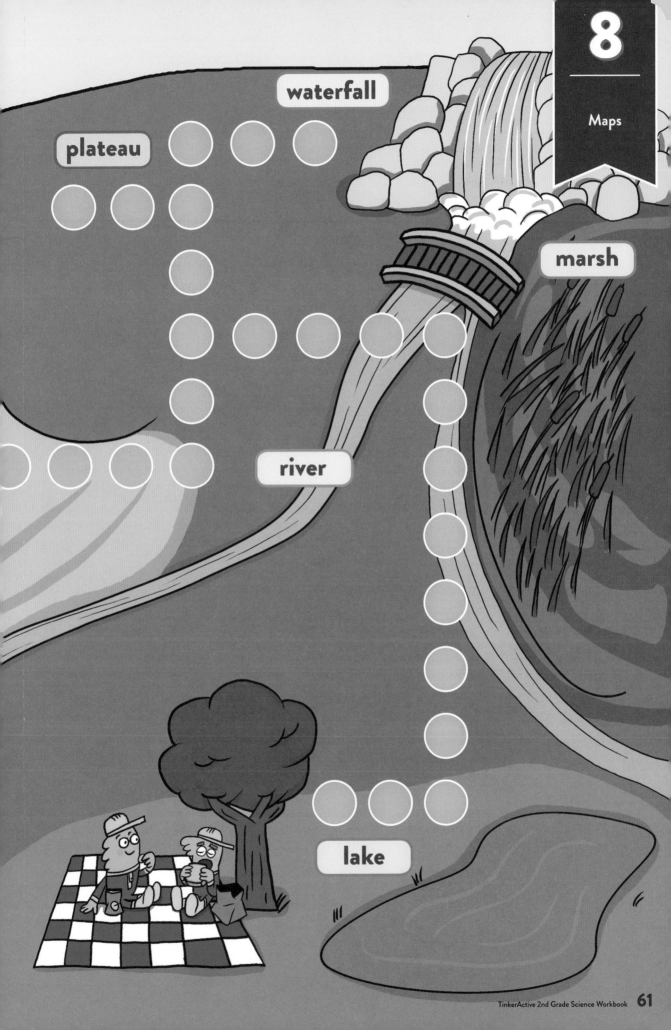

Maps often have features that help users read and decode the information. Look at this map and read the title, key, scale, and compass.

MAKER CITY

Key

road

orchard

sea

lighthouse

city hall

sports field

Scale

0   5   10

1 inch = 10 miles

Compass

N

W   E

S

Draw a map of your home. Include a title, a key, and any other features you need on your map.

_____

Title

Key

LET'S START!

GATHER THESE TOOLS AND MATERIALS.

Cups

Cereal boxes or cardboard boxes

Small items like:
leaves, coins, toothpicks, buttons,
cotton balls, rocks, and dice

Toilet paper or paper towel rolls

Aluminum foil

LET'S TINKER!

Use your materials to represent different features of your neighborhood. For example, a cup turned upside down can represent a hill.

- Which materials can represent natural features like land, water, and trees?
- Which materials can represent man-made features like bridges, roads, and buildings?
- How can you use your materials alone or assembled together?

LET'S MAKE: DREAM ISLAND MAP

Make and draw a map of your own imaginary island. **Choose** materials that can be used to show the edges of the island and different landforms. Which materials can represent the water—both the water around your island and any features like a river, lake, or waterfall? What else is on your island? A city? A volcano?

LET'S ENGINEER!

Amelia is designing her dream playground for a new park in her neighborhood. Her playground will be very large—so large, MotMots might get lost!

How can Amelia show others where everything is?

Draw a map of your dream playground. **Use** the materials to show the natural and man-made features you will include.

How can you be sure that other people can read your map correctly? **Show** your map to someone else and ask questions about what they see.

PROJECT 8: DONE!
Get your sticker!

Underwater Habitats

There are many different types of underwater habitats on Earth. The oceans, Earth's biggest habitat, are filled with salt water. Most lakes, rivers, ponds, and wetlands are freshwater habitats. Each type of underwater habitat has great diversity, which means different kinds of plants and animals live there.

Read about each animal. Then draw a line to its freshwater habitat.

Lake sturgeon are big fish. They can weigh up to 200 pounds and live in big, open bodies of water.

The **electric eel** lives in rivers. It makes an electric current to shock its prey.

The **bowfin** is also called a mudfish because it can live in shallow, muddy water.

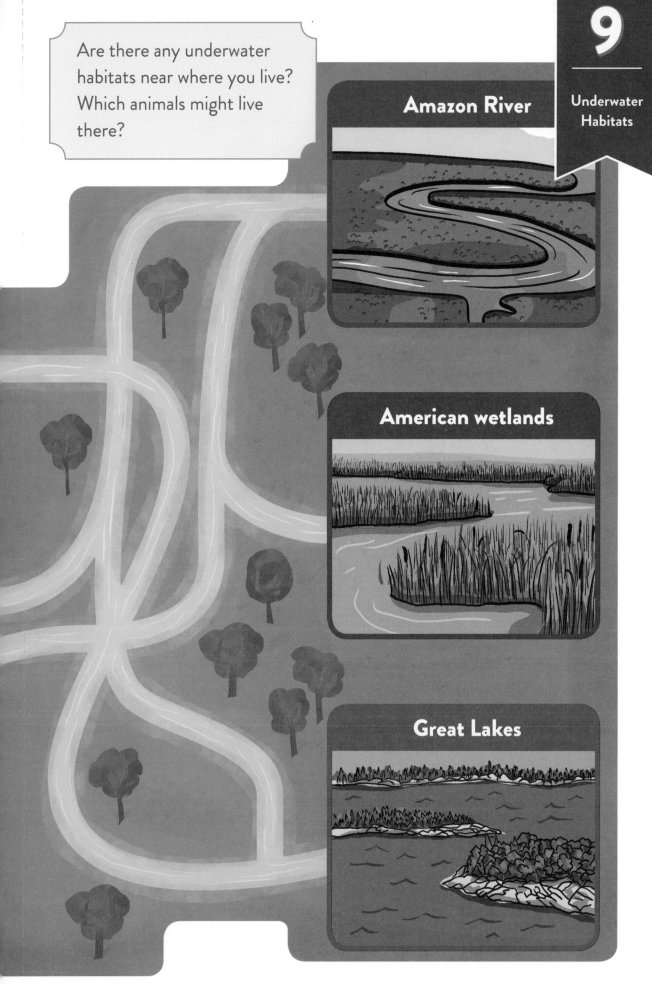

Are there any underwater habitats near where you live? Which animals might live there?

Amazon River

American wetlands

Great Lakes

The Great Barrier Reef is a saltwater ocean habitat off Australia. It is an enormous, colorful coral reef that thousands of plants and animals call home. Over a hundred different species of sharks live in the Great Barrier Reef habitat!

Read the poem aloud.

Zebra Stripes

I see a spotted zebra shark—
It doesn't have any stripes!
Why is it called that animal?
Spots are on many other types.

The zebra shark wraps its eggs,
In a very special case.
It's called a mermaid's purse,
And it holds the eggs in place.

The baby shark grows inside,
Until it's time to hatch.
Then the zebra shark pup is born—
With zebra stripes to match!

Look at the different sharks in this picture. Then draw a line connecting your two favorite sharks.

How are they the same?

_____

_____

How are they different?

_____

_____

A shark can lose hundreds, or even thousands, of teeth in its lifetime. Can you find eleven lost shark's teeth?

There are many different habitats at all levels of the ocean. There are tide pools along the shore, kelp forests underwater, seafloor trenches so deep people have never explored them, and many others.

Look at the levels of the ocean. Draw a line to lead the submarine to the the ocean trench.

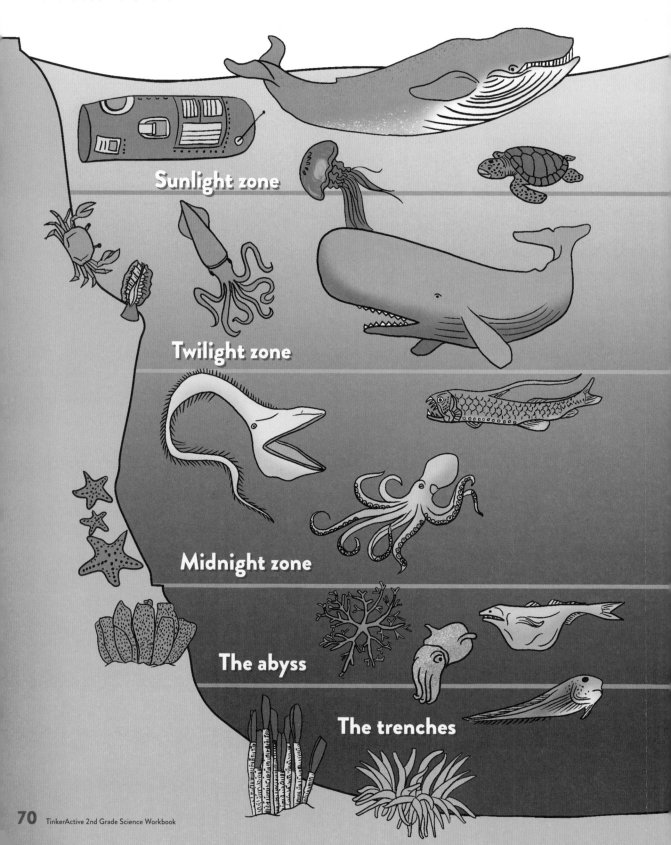

Sunlight zone

Twilight zone

Midnight zone

The abyss

The trenches

Two of these ocean creatures are real, but one is made up. Cross out the animal you predict is not real, and write about how you came to this conclusion.

The **dumbo octopus** has two fins that look like ears. The octopus flaps these fins to move. It swims along the seafloor looking for snails, worms, and other food.

The **fangtooth fish** has giant teeth, but its entire body isn't much larger than your hand. Its teeth help it capture prey of any size that wanders its way.

The **tube shark** has rows of tubes on its back to help it blend in with tube worms on the ocean floor. It lives and hunts in the sunlight zone.

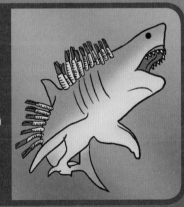

_____

_____

_____

LET'S START! GATHER THESE TOOLS AND MATERIALS.

 Flashlight	 Sheets or pillowcases	 Markers	 Paper	 6 or more drinking straws
 Scissors	 Glue	 Shoebox	 4–6 rocks	 4–6 rubber bands

LET'S TINKER!

There is plenty of bright light at the top of the ocean, but in some places, the water goes so deep that no light reaches there—it is completely dark.

Go to a dark place, like a closet. Then **use** your materials to show light and dark. If you can, **show** some shades of light in between as well.

LET'S MAKE: COLORFUL CORAL

Corals are colorful animals that live together in the ocean. They make hard outer shells that form coral reefs. Make a model of corals with your materials.

1. Color each drinking straw a different color.

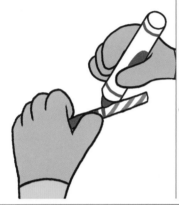

2. Cut them into small pieces.

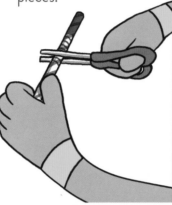

3. Glue the pieces to the paper upright like coral.

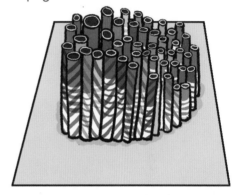

LET'S ENGINEER!

Dimitri is thinking about getting a pet goldfish. But he doesn't know what his goldfish will need, and he's worried that it won't like living with him.

How can Dimitri prepare for his goldfish?

Build a model of a fish tank using the shoebox. Think about a goldfish's natural habitat.

- What plants should live in the tank?
- Should there be other animals in it?
- Which materials can represent these plants and animals?

PROJECT 9: DONE!
Get your sticker!

Land Habitats

There are many types of land habitats, and each one is filled with unique plants and animals. The desert is a habitat that gets little rain. The plants and animals there have features and skills that help them survive with little water.

Read about each desert plant or animal. Then follow the instructions and answer each question.

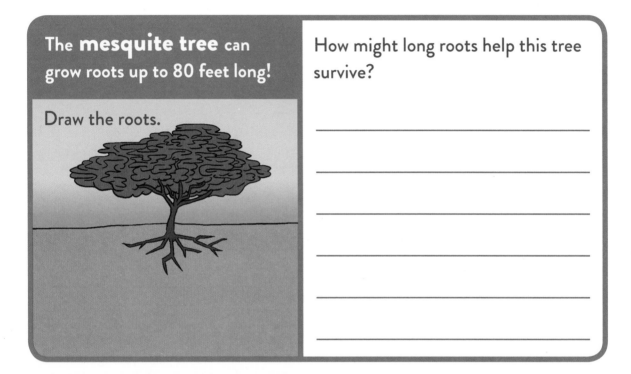

The mesquite tree can grow roots up to 80 feet long!

Draw the roots.

How might long roots help this tree survive?

_____

_____

_____

_____

_____

_____

The gila woodpecker makes a home inside a cactus.

Draw the woodpecker inside his home.

How might this home help the woodpecker survive?

_____

_____

_____

_____

_____

_____

In the desert, where food is scarce, the **dung beetle** finds something to eat—dung. It rolls the poop of other animals into balls!

How might rolling the dung into balls help the beetles survive?

Draw balls of food.

_____

_____

_____

_____

_____

_____

The **barrel cactus** has spines up to 4 inches long.

How might the spines help this cactus survive?

Draw the spines.

_____

_____

_____

_____

_____

_____

_____

_____

The rain forest is the land habitat with the greatest diversity on Earth. This means that rain forests have the largest variety of different plants and animals.

Read the travel journal aloud. Then answer each question.

Yesterday we explored the Amazon rain forest! We walked on the **forest floor** past large red and orange mushrooms. It was dark and wet—the tall trees blocked most of the light. It smelled like soggy dirt after it rains. I didn't want to run into any jaguars or anteaters! But Callie did see a bright blue poison dart frog.

Next, we climbed a wooden staircase and stepped onto a hanging walkway through the **understory**. It was hot, and I had to push a lot of giant, waxy leaves out of my way. We saw leafcutter ants marching up the smooth tree bark!

Last, we climbed over 100 feet up the **canopy**. I was tired! Lots of vines and ferns hung from the trees. I liked the sweet-smelling purple orchid flowers. There were animals all around—I could even hear monkeys squeaking, grunting, and howling! Dimitri grabbed some sweet mangoes as he walked by.

From there, I could see the very top, the **emergent layer**, where a few trees stretched 200 feet into the sky! It was bright and very hot. We watched the trees sway in the wind, but we didn't see many animals that high up.

What might you HEAR in the rain forest?

_____

_____

_____

What might you SEE in the rain forest?

_____

_____

_____

What might you TOUCH in the rain forest?

_____

_____

_____

What might you TASTE in the rain forest?

_____

_____

_____

What might you SMELL in the rain forest?

_____

_____

_____

There are grassland habitats all over the world, and they are all covered in grasses.

The MotMots went on a safari in the grasslands of South Africa and printed photos of the animals they saw. But photos from other trips got mixed in with them. Cross out the photos of animals that do not live in the grasslands.

Go on a safari outside your home. What plants and animals live near you? Draw what you observe in your habitat and write any plant or animal's name.

MY SAFARI

LET'S START! GATHER THESE TOOLS AND MATERIALS.

Jar with a lid

Sand and dirt

Rocks

Moss or small plants

Cereal boxes or cardboard boxes

Water

Aluminum foil

LET'S TINKER!

Earth has a great diversity of plants and animals—each type of living thing is unique.

Think about how your materials are alike and how they are different. Then **sort** them by a trait like color, texture, or size. What other ways can the materials be sorted?

LET'S MAKE: MINI RAIN FOREST

1. Using a clear jar with a lid, **place** a layer of sand and rocks in the jar.

2. Add dirt on top, piling it high on the sides.

3. Put moss and/or small plants on top.

4. Carefully **add** water to the lowest part of the jar to make a "lake" next to the "mountain" of dirt and rocks. **Close** the lid.

5. Check back in a day, several days, and then a week. How does it change?

LET'S ENGINEER!

Callie's friends the dung beetles are rolling their food into balls so they can move them around and store them easily. They want to move the balls to the other side of the yard, but a large stone wall is in the way. Callie wants to help, but she doesn't want to touch the dung balls.

How can Callie help her friends without touching the dung balls?

Crumple some aluminum foil into balls to represent the dung balls. **Think** about how you might try to push objects up and over something. **Use** your materials to make something that helps the dung beetles push their balls up and over the stone wall.

PROJECT 10: DONE!
Get your sticker!

Plant Growth

Plants need air, sunlight, water, and nutrients from the dirt to grow. They have specialized parts to help meet their needs.

Dimitri is taking pictures of his garden. Label the part of a plant that you see in each picture.

roots	**leaves**	**trunk**	**fruit**
stem	**flower**	**branches**	**seeds**

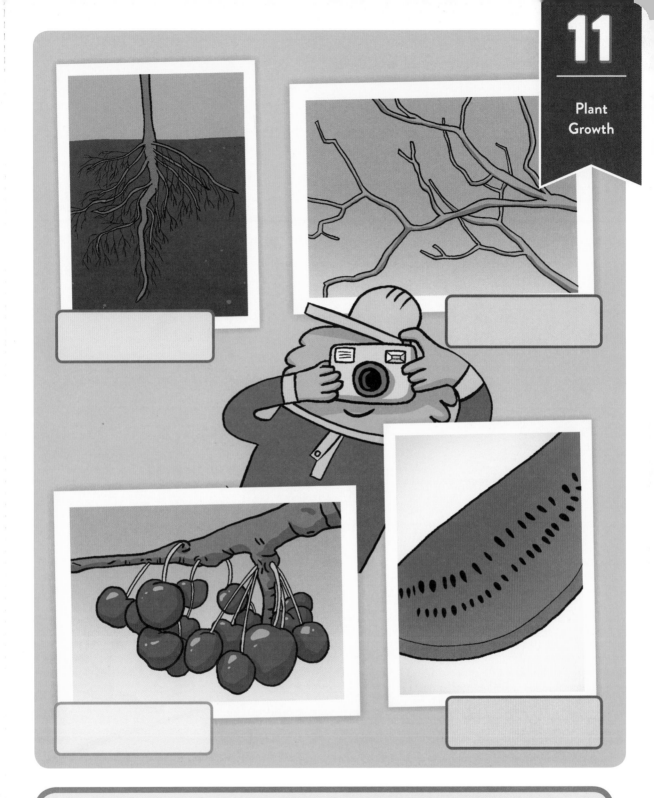

Circle the plant part that soaks up water and nutrients from the ground.

Draw a triangle around the plant part that collects sunlight and makes food for the plant.

Draw a rectangle around the plant part that protects seeds.

Read the poem about a seed aloud.

A Place to Grow

Hello there!
I'm a dandelion seed.
Can you tell me where to go?
I'm just floating in the wind,
Looking for a place to grow.

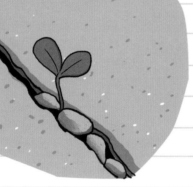

I needed a bit of dirt—
I found enough for me!
My roots will dig down deep.
Water and nutrients are key.

I know I need some sunlight—
What keeps blocking out the sun?
I reach high between the shadows,
But then comes another one!

Describe a habitat near your home where a dandelion seed could get all the air, sunlight, water, and nutrients it needs to grow.

_____

_____

_____

_____

Draw a line to match each plant to the habitat where it grows.

The **oak tree** has thick bark to protect the water inside while living in a dry habitat.

Cattails have fast-growing roots to anchor them in moving water.

Seagrass has many wide leaves to absorb the sunlight in shallow water.

Predict what will happen at the end of each experiment.

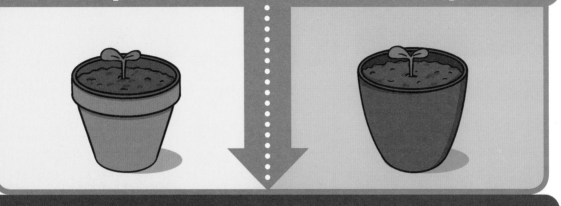

Callie plants two seeds in two pots.

Then she covers one plant so it won't get any light.

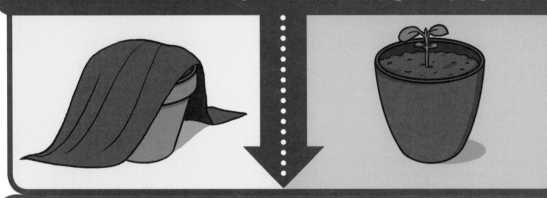

Plants collect sunlight with their leaves to make food. They do that by using chlorophyll, which keeps their leaves green. Plants need sunlight to make them grow.

Draw your prediction.

Brian plants two seeds in two pots.

Then he stops watering one plant.

Plants soak up water with their roots. Then the water travels to the leaves, where it helps to make food. Plants need water to make food and to keep from drying out.

Draw your prediction.

Look for plants inside or outside your home. Where do they get the sunlight and water that they need?

LET'S START! GATHER THESE TOOLS AND MATERIALS.

Paper

Scissors

20 or more
drinking straws

Piece of string
2–3 feet long

Paper
towel roll

Tape

Glue

Crayons

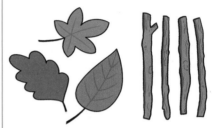
Sticks and leaves

LET'S TINKER!

Leaves come in all shapes, sizes, and colors. Leaves are important to plants because they gather light and make food.

Cut paper to make different leaf shapes and color them. What other materials can you add to your leaves to make them look more real?

LET'S MAKE: PLANT PARTS

1. **Cut** and glue pieces of straws or string onto paper to represent plant roots.

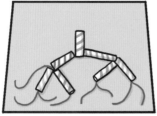

2. **Glue** on a paper towel roll to represent a stem or trunk.

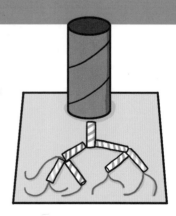

3. Draw a line to represent the ground.

4. Does your plant have branches, leaves, a flower, or a fruit? What other parts can you make and add? **Put** them all together to complete your plant.

LET'S ENGINEER!

The tall tree in Enid's yard loves sunlight—and Enid loves her tree. She wants to show her classmates how it uses its roots, trunk, and branches to hold its leaves up high, where the sunlight can reach them.

How can Enid show her classmates how her tree works?

Make a model of a tree. **Use** only your drinking straws as a trunk and branches. **Use** tape to connect the straws. **Choose** the best material to represent roots.

- How can you connect the straws to build a strong base like a trunk?

- How can you keep your tree from falling over, like roots do for plants?

- Can you build your tree as tall as your knee? Or taller?

PROJECT 11: DONE!
Get your sticker!

Plant Pollination

Plants grow in one place and can't move. They need help with pollination—moving pollen between flowering plants of the same type to make seeds. Wind, water, and animals all help pollinate plants and spread their seeds.

Read about how each animal helps flowers pollinate. Then draw a line to lead each animal from one flower to the flower bush.

Bees collect nectar and pollen from flowers to make honey. As they fly from flower to flower, they spread pollen.

Hummingbirds can drink nectar from over 1,000 flowers a day! Pollen sticks to their beaks and is spread to new flowers.

How do you think wind or water helps spread pollen?

_____

_____

_____

When **butterflies** drink nectar from flowers, pollen sticks to their legs, tongues, and bodies. They can spread the pollen over long distances as they fly.

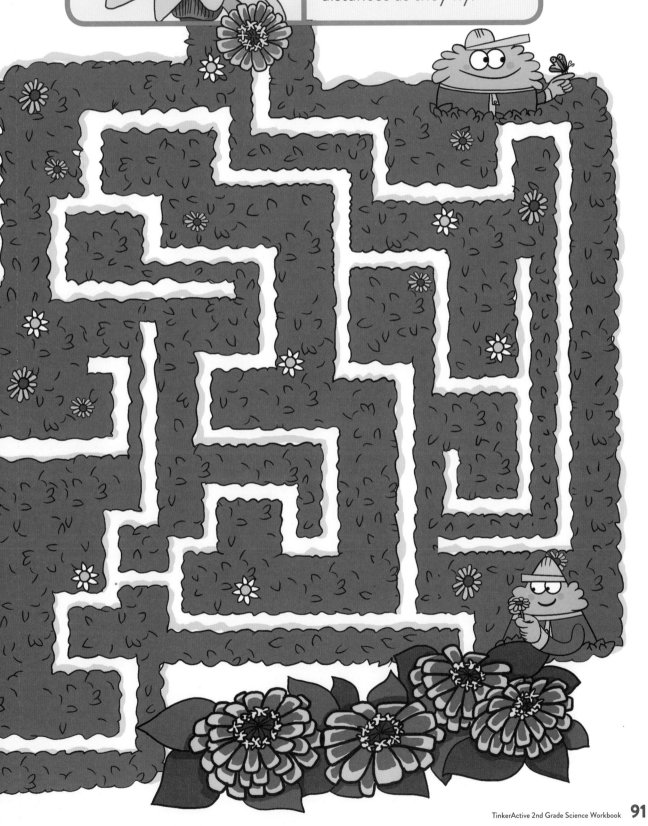

Read aloud some of the ways that animals can move seeds. Then draw a line to match each method to an animal.

Some animals eat fruits and vegetables full of seeds. Later, when they poop, the seeds are left on the ground to grow new plants.

Some animals move seeds around when they store their food. They might even bury seeds underground. If they forget about the seeds, new plants grow.

Some animals get burs full of seeds stuck in their fur. Then the burs fall off in other places to grow new plants.

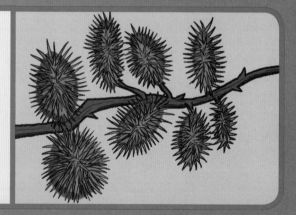

Draw your own bur—a seed with a sticky or spiky covering. Then draw a line to an animal that could help move it.

SQUIRREL

LIZARD

BEAR

Wind and water also help move and spread seeds. Circle the seeds you predict can spread by flying, floating, or even spinning in the wind.

Draw what you predict happens when the wind blows by a dandelion.

People can also move seeds. Look in your kitchen for fruits and vegetables. Write about and draw the fruits and vegetables with seeds that your family has moved.

_____

_____

_____

Draw the inside and outside of your favorite fruit or favorite vegetable. Circle the seeds. Then write whether the seeds are on the inside or outside.

_____

LET'S START!

GATHER THESE TOOLS AND MATERIALS.

Tissue paper

4–6 twist ties

4–6 paper clips

4–6 toothpicks

Paper

Scissors

LET'S TINKER!

Which materials can move like a seed in the wind? **Make** your materials float, fly, or spin.

Change or combine your materials to alter how they move.

Make a seed that sticks like a bur and is ready to go for a ride!

Choose or make materials that act like spines or small hooks that will attach to your shirt or hair.

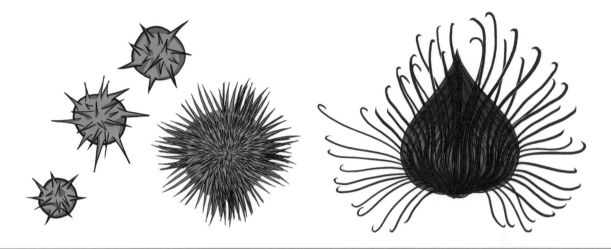

LET'S ENGINEER!

Enid is throwing a birthday party for Frank! She wants a big celebration with balloons and the best confetti. She wants the confetti to move through the air in different ways—parachuting, flying on wings, twisting, twirling, gliding, and fluttering.

How can Enid make confetti that moves through the air in different ways?

Cut your paper into small pieces to make confetti. **Think** about how seeds fly in different ways. What can you do to your paper to make it more like those different seeds? **Try** a few designs. Could any of your other materials be added to help?

PROJECT 12: DONE!
Get your sticker!

Engineering Design: Shoe

It's time to go to lunch, but Amelia is having trouble with one of her shoes. Why?

RESEARCH THE PROBLEM!

OBSERVE

What do you notice
about the shoe?

_____

_____

_____

GATHER
INFORMATION

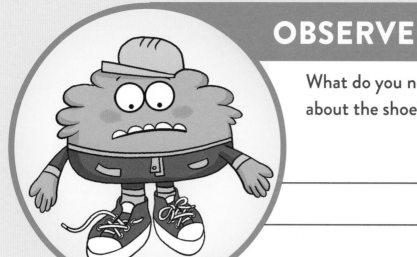

What can you learn by touching
the shoe?

_____

_____

_____

ASK QUESTIONS

What would you ask Amelia about
her shoe?

_____

_____

_____

Look at the picture. Why isn't Amelia's shoe tied?

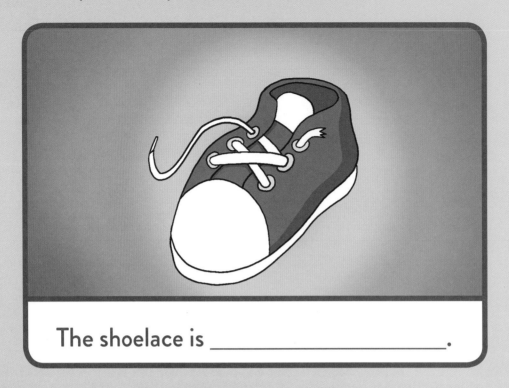

The shoelace is _____.

What caused the problem? Write about and draw possible causes.

Think about possible solutions for Amelia's problem. Then write about and draw an idea that can fix the problem.

What can the MotMots **do** that might help Amelia? Write about and draw a solution.

What materials can Amelia **use** to fix the shoe? Write about and draw a solution.

What can Amelia **do** to fix the shoe? Write about and draw a solution.

Each possible solution to a problem has strong points and weak points. You can compare solutions to choose the best design. Choose two solutions from the previous page to test. Write a name for each solution and follow the directions.

Solution 1: _____

Draw one solution and what you think will happen when Amelia tries to walk to lunch.

What works?

_____

_____

_____

What doesn't work?

_____

_____

_____

How can you fix what doesn't work or improve your design?

_____

_____

Solution 2: _____

Draw the other solution and what you think will happen when Amelia tries to walk to lunch.

What works?

_____

_____

_____

What doesn't work?

_____

_____

_____

How can you fix what doesn't work or improve your design?

_____

_____

Circle the solution you think Amelia should use.

LET'S START!

Aluminum foil

Tape

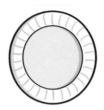
Paper plate

Pencil, marker, or crayon

Cardboard
(about the size of a piece of paper)

String

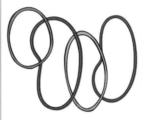
4–6 rubber bands

Stuffed animal

LET'S TINKER!

Look at your materials. How can they be worn? **Try** making a bracelet, hat, helmet, belt, crown, or even armor. How can the materials be combined to make something that you can wear?

LET'S MAKE: MOTMOT SHOES

A shoe is made of many parts working together.

1. Choose materials that are strong enough to walk on the ground like the soles of shoes do.

2. Trace your feet on the material and cut them out.

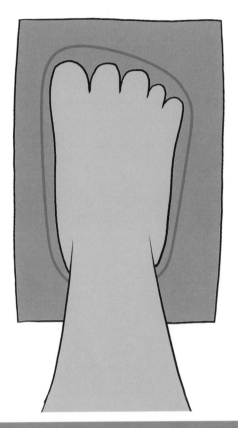

3. Make a cover for each foot as the top of the shoe. You can **add** stickers from page 129 to decorate your shoes.

4. Add materials like rubber bands or string to hold the parts together and to keep the shoes on your feet—like laces or straps!

LET'S ENGINEER!

Frank loves taking his best friend, MotBot, to the park. But his robot's feet keep getting dirty!

How can Frank protect MotBot's feet?

Use a stuffed animal or doll as a model for MotBot. Then **use** your materials to protect your toy's feet.

- How can you combine the materials to keep its feet clean?
- What happens to the "shoes" when you pick up your stuffed animal or doll?
- How will your invention stay on the toy as you play?

PROJECT 13: DONE!
Get your sticker!

Engineering Design: Fountain

The MotMots are thirsty from playing.
They would like a drink from the water fountain,
but no water is coming out. Why?

RESEARCH THE PROBLEM!

OBSERVE

What do you notice about the water fountain?

_____

_____

GATHER INFORMATION

What can you learn by touching the water fountain?

_____

_____

ASK QUESTIONS

What can you ask the MotMots about the water fountain or the environment?

_____

_____

_____

Look at the picture. Why isn't the fountain on?

The fountain is_____.

What caused the problem? Write about and draw possible causes.

Think about possible solutions for the MotMots' problem.
Then write about and draw an idea that can fix the problem.

What can the MotMots **do** that might help? Write about and draw a solution.

What materials can the MotMots **use** that might help? Write about and draw a solution.

What can the MotMots **bring** to the park that might help? Write about and draw a solution.

Each possible solution to a problem has strong points and weak points. You can compare solutions to choose the best design. Choose two solutions from the previous page to test. Write a name for each solution and follow the directions.

Solution 1: _____

Draw one solution and what you think will happen the next time the MotMots press the fountain's button for a drink.

What works?

_____

_____

_____

What doesn't work?

_____

_____

_____

How can you fix what doesn't work or improve your design?

_____

_____

Solution 2: _____

Draw the other solution and what you think will happen the next time the MotMots press the fountain's button for a drink.

What works?

_____

_____

_____

What doesn't work?

_____

_____

_____

How can you fix what doesn't work or improve your design?

_____

_____

Circle the solution you think the MotMots should use.

LET'S START! GATHER THESE TOOLS AND MATERIALS.

Sandwich bag	 Aluminum foil	 4–6 drinking straws
 Plastic wrap	 Rubber bands	 Tall, clear drinking glass

Assorted liquids
(with an adult's help):

- honey (or maple syrup)
- milk
- dish soap
- water
- vegetable oil
- rubbing alcohol

LET'S TINKER!

Dip or dunk the sandwich bag, aluminum foil, straws, plastic wrap, and rubber bands in water. What happens?

- How does the water react when you jiggle or tilt the materials?
- Do any of the materials absorb the water?

Shake the water off these materials to see if you can get them dry.

LET'S MAKE: LIQUID RAINBOW

Some liquids are denser and heavier than water. Make a rainbow with liquids of different densities!

1. **Pour** about 1 inch of honey into the glass without pouring any on the sides.

2. Slowly **add** about 1 inch of each of the rest of the liquids, in this order: milk, dish soap, and then water. Don't pour any of the liquids on the sides of the glass.

3. Slowly **pour** the last two liquids down the sides of the glass, in this order: vegetable oil and then rubbing alcohol. Because these are the lightest liquids, pour them slowly.

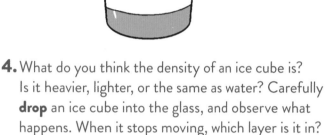

4. What do you think the density of an ice cube is? Is it heavier, lighter, or the same as water? Carefully **drop** an ice cube into the glass, and observe what happens. When it stops moving, which layer is it in?

TIP: If any of the layers were poured too quickly, let the glass sit for a bit and the liquids will settle into a rainbow (with no mixing of the layers).

LET'S ENGINEER!

Callie is going on a hike, but she can't find her water bottle!

How can Callie carry water with her?

Choose materials that can hold water and design a container for Callie to use. **Think** about the features of a water bottle.

- How can Callie get water in and out of her container?
- How will Callie drink from it?
- Do you need more than one material?

PROJECT 14: DONE!
Get your sticker!

Engineering Design: Slide

It's a busy day at the playground.
But no one is using the slide. Why?

RESEARCH THE PROBLEM!

OBSERVE

What do you notice about the slide?

_____

_____

GATHER INFORMATION

What might you learn by touching the slide?

_____

_____

ASK QUESTIONS

What would you ask the MotMots about the slide?

_____

_____

Look at the picture. Why aren't the MotMots playing on the slide?

The slide is_____.

What caused the problem? Write about and draw possible causes.

Think about possible solutions for the MotMots' problem. Then write about and draw an idea that can fix the problem.

What can the MotMots **wear** so they can use the slide? Write about and draw a solution.

What materials **can** the MotMots **use** so they can go down the slide? Write about and draw a solution.

What can the MotMots **build** so they can use the slide? Write about and draw a solution.

Each possible solution to a problem has strong points and weak points. You can compare solutions to choose the best design. Choose two solutions from the previous page to test. Write a name for each solution and follow the directions.

Solution 1: _____

Draw one solution and what you think will happen the next time the MotMots play at the playground.

What works?

_____

_____

_____

What doesn't work?

_____

_____

_____

How can you fix what doesn't work or improve your design?

_____

_____

Solution 2: _____

Draw the other solution and what you think will happen the next time the MotMots play at the playground.

What works?

_____

_____

_____

What doesn't work?

_____

_____

_____

How can you fix what doesn't work or improve your design?

_____

_____

Circle the solution you think the MotMots should use.

LET'S START!

Aluminum foil

Toilet paper rolls and/or paper towel rolls

Tape

Marble
(or other small rolling object)

Cardboard

Books

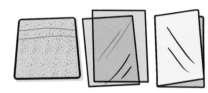

Flat materials like:
washcloth, waxed paper, and napkin

LET'S TINKER!

A slide is made of many materials that have unique properties. Which of these materials is slippery like a slide?

- How can you tell?
- Are any reflective?

Test each one by sliding a book or other small objects across them.

LET'S MAKE: MARBLE SLIDE

A slide is an inclined plane—its surface is tilted at an angle so things slide down it. Make a slide using inclined planes.

1. Tape a toilet paper roll or paper towel roll to a wall, tilted at an angle.

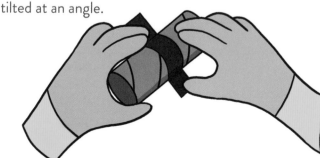

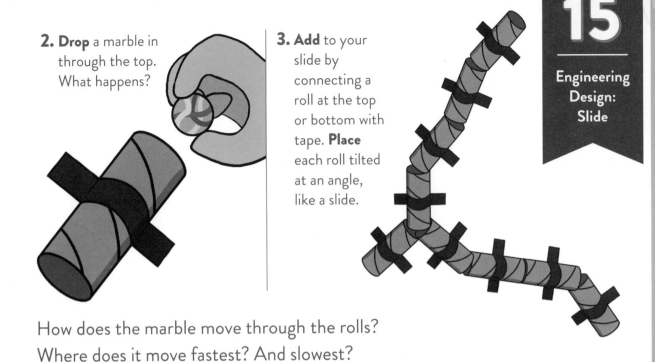

2. Drop a marble in through the top. What happens?

3. Add to your slide by connecting a roll at the top or bottom with tape. **Place** each roll tilted at an angle, like a slide.

How does the marble move through the rolls? Where does it move fastest? And slowest?

LET'S ENGINEER!

The school is getting a new slide for the school playground. Amelia is in charge of choosing the material the slide will be made of.

How can she choose the best material for the slide?

Compare and test different materials for a slide. First, **create** an inclined plane, like a slide. **Place** a piece of cardboard at an angle by holding one side up with books and taping the bottom. Next, **cover** the slide with a material such as foil. Last, **test** the slide. **Drop** a marble from the top. How does it move?

- Is it fast or slow?
- Bumpy or smooth?

Test more materials for covering the slide to see how they perform. What type of material makes the best surface for the new slide? Which materials do not make a good surface for sliding?

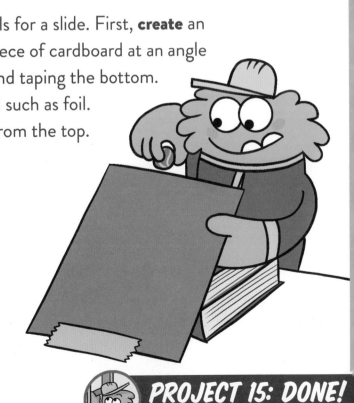

PROJECT 15: DONE!
Get your sticker!

ANSWER KEY

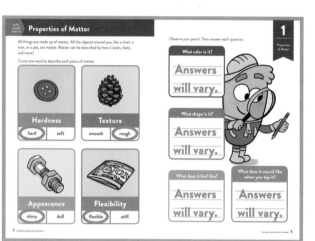

Properties of Matter

All things are made up of matter. All the objects around you, like a chair, a tree, or a pet, are matter. Matter can be described by how it looks, feels, and more!

Circle one word to describe each piece of matter.

Hardness — hard / soft
Texture — smooth / rough
Appearance — shiny / dull
Flexibility — flexible / stiff

Observe your pencil. Then answer each question.

What color is it?
Answers will vary.

What shape is it?
Answers will vary.

What does it feel like?
Answers will vary.

What does it sound like when you tap it?
Answers will vary.

Matter has different properties – for example, paper is thin, while a tree trunk is thick. Because of these differences, different types of matter are useful for different needs.

Read the text aloud. Then circle the object that each MotMot needs and explain why you chose that object.

Enid needs a flexible material to wrap her trophy in.
Why? Answers will vary.

Brian needs a soft material to clean this mirror with.
Why? Answers will vary.

Frank needs a strong material to make a leash for his pet alligator.
Why? Answers will vary.

Dimitri needs a heavy material to hold open this door.
Why? Answers will vary.

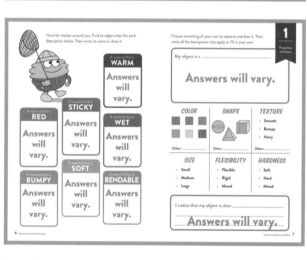

Hunt for matter around you. Find an object that fits each description below. Then write its name or draw it.

A material that is WARM — Answers will vary.
A material that is RED — Answers will vary.
A material that is WET — Answers will vary.
A material that is STICKY — Answers will vary.
A material that is BUMPY — Answers will vary.
A material that is SOFT — Answers will vary.
A material that is BENDABLE — Answers will vary.

Choose something of your own to observe and draw it. Then circle all the descriptions that apply or fill in your own.

My object is a _____
Answers will vary.

COLOR
SHAPE
TEXTURE
- Smooth
- Bumpy
- Hairy
Other: ___

SIZE
- Small
- Medium
- Large
FLEXIBILITY
- Flexible
- Rigid
- Mixed
HARDNESS
- Soft
- Hard
- Mixed

I notice that my object is also: _____
Answers will vary.

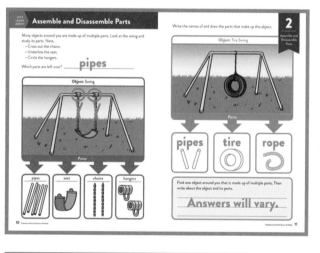

Assemble and Disassemble Parts

Many objects around you are made up of multiple parts. Look at the swing and study its parts. Next,
- Cross out the chains.
- Underline the seat.
- Circle the hangers.

Which parts are left over? **pipes**

Object: Swing
Parts: pipes, seat, chains, hangers

Write the names of and draw the parts that make up this object.

Object: Tire Swing
Parts: pipes, tire, rope

Find one object around you that is made up of multiple parts. Then write about the object and its parts.
Answers will vary.

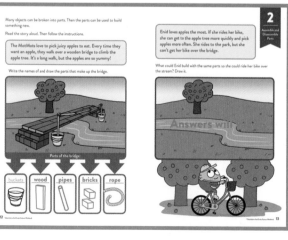

Many objects can be broken into parts. Then the parts can be used to build something new.

Read the story aloud. Then follow the instructions.

The MotMots love to pick juicy apples to eat. Every time they want an apple, they walk over a wooden bridge to climb the apple tree. It's a long walk, but the apples are so yummy!

Write the names of and draw the parts that make up the bridge.

Parts of the bridge: buckets, wood, pipes, bricks, rope

Enid loves apples the most. If she rides her bike, she can get to the apple tree more quickly and pick apples more often. She rides to the park, but she can't get her bike over the bridge.

What could Enid build with the same parts so she could ride her bike over the stream? Draw it.
Answers will vary.

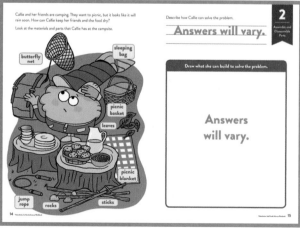

Callie and her friends are camping. They want to picnic, but it looks like it will rain soon. How can Callie keep her friends and the food dry?

Look at the materials and parts that Callie has at the campsite.

butterfly net, sleeping bag, picnic basket, leaves, picnic blanket, jump rope, rocks, sticks

Describe how Callie can solve the problem.
Answers will vary.

Draw what she can build to solve the problem.
Answers will vary.

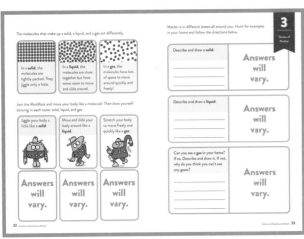

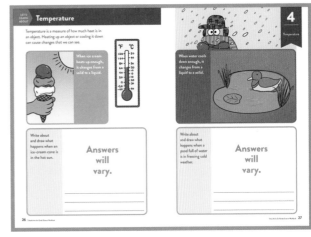

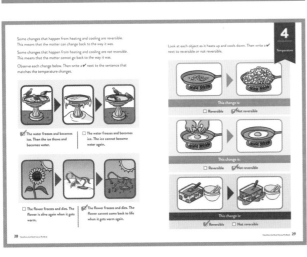

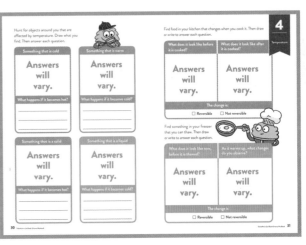

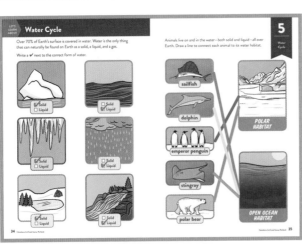

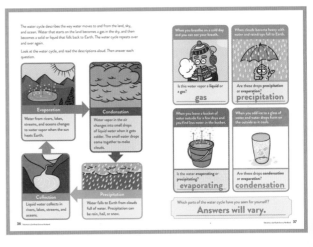

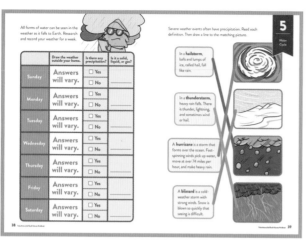

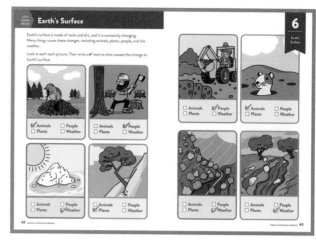

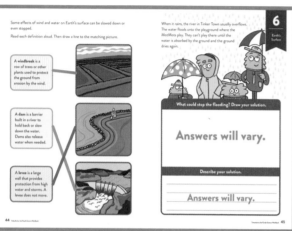

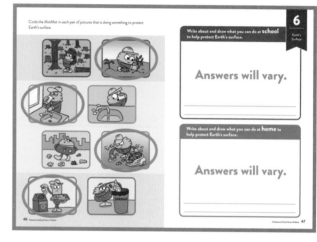

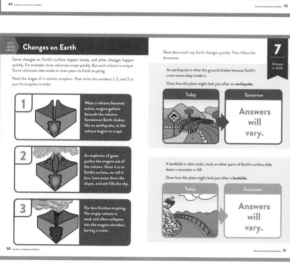

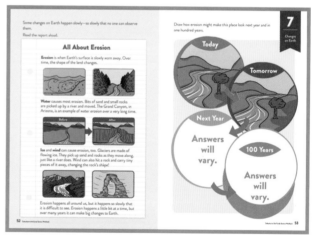

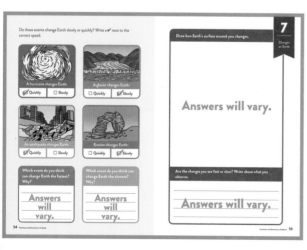

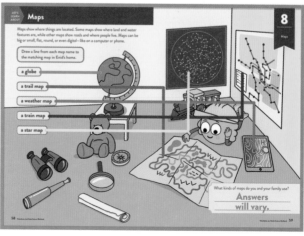

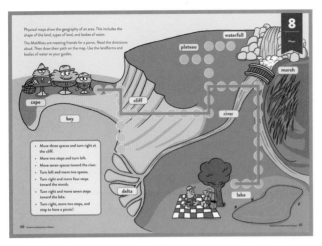

Physical maps show the geography of an area. This includes the shape of the land, types of land, and bodies of water.

The MotMots are meeting friends for a picnic. Read the directions aloud. Then draw their path on the map. Use the landforms and bodies of water as your guides.

8
Maps

waterfall
plateau
marsh
cape
cliff
river
bay
delta
lake

- Move three spaces and turn right at the cliff.
- Move two steps and turn left.
- Move seven spaces toward the river.
- Turn left and move two spaces.
- Turn right and move four steps toward the marsh.
- Turn right and move seven steps toward the lake.
- Turn right, move two steps, and stop to have a picnic!

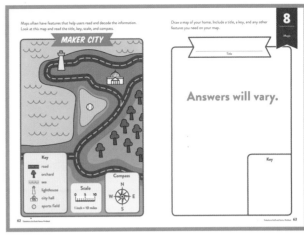

Maps often have features that help users read and decode the information. Look at this map and read the title, key, scale, and compass.

Draw a map of your home. Include a title, a key, and any other features you need on your map.

8
Maps

MAKER CITY

Answers will vary.

Key
road
orchard
sea
lighthouse
city hall
sports field

Scale
0 5 10
1 inch = 10 miles

Compass
N W E S

Title

Key

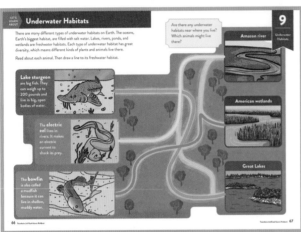

LET'S LEARN ABOUT
Underwater Habitats

9
Underwater Habitats

There are many different types of underwater habitats on Earth. The oceans, Earth's biggest habitat, are filled with salt water. Lakes, rivers, ponds, and wetlands are freshwater habitats. Each type of underwater habitat has great diversity, which means different kinds of plants and animals live there.

Read about each animal. Then draw a line to its freshwater habitat.

Are there any underwater habitats near where you live? Which animals might live there?

Amazon river
American wetlands
Great Lakes

Lake sturgeon are big fish. They can weigh up to 200 pounds and live in big, open bodies of water.

The **electric eel** lives in rivers. It makes an electric current to shock its prey.

The **bowfin** is also called a mudfish because it can live in shallow, muddy water.

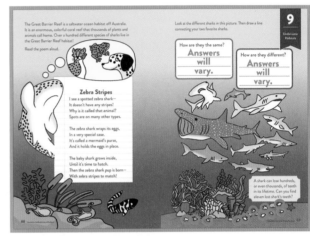

9
Underwater Habitats

The Great Barrier Reef is a saltwater ocean habitat off Australia. It is an enormous, colorful coral reef that thousands of plants and animals call home. Over a hundred different species of sharks live in the Great Barrier Reef too!

Read the poem aloud.

Look at the different sharks in this picture. Then draw a line connecting your two favorite sharks.

How are they the same?
Answers will vary.

How are they different?
Answers will vary.

Zebra Stripes
I see a spotted zebra shark—
It doesn't have any stripes!
Why is it called that animal?
Spots are on many other types.

The zebra shark wraps its eggs,
In a very special case.
It's called a mermaid's purse,
And it holds the eggs in place.

The baby shark grows inside,
Until it's time to hatch.
Then the zebra shark pup is born—
With zebra stripes to match!

A shark can lose hundreds, or even thousands, of teeth in its lifetime. Can you find eleven lost shark's teeth?

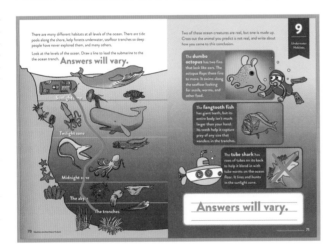

There are many different habitats at all levels of the ocean. There are tide pools along the shore, kelp forests underwater, seafloor trenches so deep people have never explored them, and many others.

Look at the levels of the ocean. Draw a line to lead the submarine to the ocean trench. **Answers will vary.**

9
Underwater Habitats

Two of these ocean creatures are real, but one is made up. Cross out the animal you predict is not real, and write about how you came to this conclusion.

Sunlight zone
Twilight zone
Midnight zone
The abyss
The trenches

The **dumbo octopus** has two fins that look like ears. The octopus flaps these fins to move. It swims along the seafloor looking for snails, worms, and other food.

The **fangtooth fish** has giant teeth, but its entire body isn't much larger than your hand. Its teeth help it capture prey of any size that wanders in the trenches.

The **tube shark** has rows of tubes on its back to help it blend in with tube worms on the ocean floor. It lives and hunts in the sunlight zone.

Answers will vary.

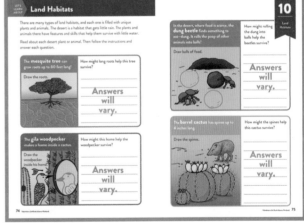

LET'S LEARN ABOUT
Land Habitats

10
Land Habitats

There are many types of land habitats, and each one is filled with unique plants and animals. The desert is a habitat that gets little rain. The plants and animals there have features and skills that help them survive with little water.

Read about each desert plant or animal. Then follow the instructions and answer each question.

The **mesquite tree** can grow roots up to 80 feet long!
Draw the roots.
How might long roots help this tree survive?
Answers will vary.

The **gila woodpecker** makes a home inside a cactus.
Draw the woodpecker inside his home.
How might this home help the woodpecker survive?
Answers will vary.

In the desert, where food is scarce, the **dung beetle** finds something to eat—dung. It rolls the poop of other animals into balls!
Draw balls of food.
How might rolling the dung into balls help the beetles survive?
Answers will vary.

The **barrel cactus** has spines up to 4 inches long.
Draw the spines.
How might the spines help this cactus survive?
Answers will vary.

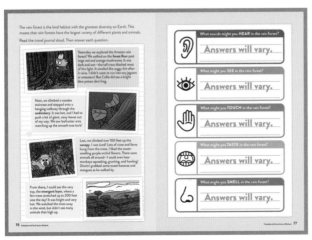

The rain forest is the land habitat with the greatest diversity on Earth. This means that rain forests have the largest variety of different plants and animals.

Read the travel journal aloud. Then answer each question.

Yesterday we explored the Amazon rain forest! We walked on the **forest floor** past large red and orange mushrooms. It was dark and wet—the tall trees blocked most of the light. It smelled like soggy dirt after it rains. I didn't want to run into any jaguars or anteaters! But Callie did see a bright blue poison dart frog.

Next, we climbed a wooden staircase and stepped into a hanging walkway through the **understory**. It was hot, and I had to push a lot of giant, waxy leaves out of my way. We saw leafcutter ants marching up the smooth tree bark!

Last, we climbed over 100 feet up the **canopy**. I was tired! Lots of vines and ferns hung from the trees. I liked the sweet-smelling purple orchid flowers. There were animals all around—I could even hear monkeys squeaking, grunting, and howling! Dimitri grabbed some sweet bananas and mangoes as he walked by.

From there, I could see the very top, the **emergent layer**, where a few trees stretched up 200 feet into the sky! It was bright and very hot. We watched the trees sway in the wind, but didn't see many animals that high up.

What sounds might you **HEAR** in the rain forest?
Answers will vary.

What might you **SEE** in the rain forest?
Answers will vary.

What might you **TOUCH** in the rain forest?
Answers will vary.

What might you **TASTE** in the rain forest?
Answers will vary.

What might you **SMELL** in the rain forest?
Answers will vary.

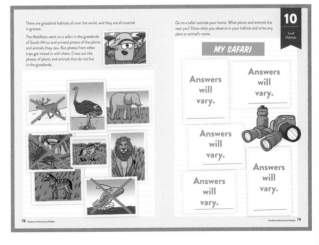

There are grassland habitats all over the world, and they are all covered in grasses.

The MotMots went on a safari in the grasslands of South Africa and printed photos of the plants and animals they saw. But photos from other trips got mixed in with them. Cross out the photos of plants and animals that do not live in the grasslands.

Go on a safari outside your home. What plants and animals live near you? Draw what you observe in your habitat and write any plant or animal's name.

10
Land Habitats

MY SAFARI

Answers will vary.
Answers will vary.
Answers will vary.
Answers will vary.

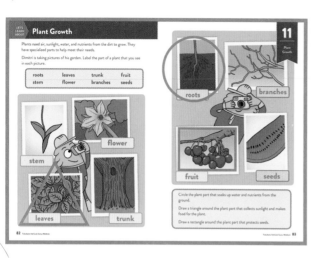

Plant Growth

Plants need air, sunlight, water, and nutrients from the dirt to grow. They have specialized parts to help meet their needs.

Dimitri is taking pictures of his garden. Label the part of a plant that you see in each picture.

roots · leaves · trunk · fruit · stem · flower · branches · seeds

stem · flower · leaves · trunk · roots · branches · fruit · seeds

Circle the plant part that soaks up water and nutrients from the ground.

Draw a triangle around the plant part that collects sunlight and makes food for the plant.

Draw a rectangle around the plant part that protects seeds.

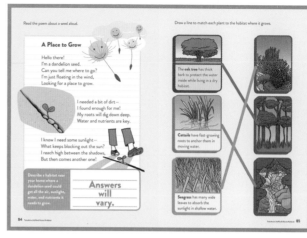

Read the poem about a seed aloud.

A Place to Grow

Hello there!
I'm a dandelion seed.
Can you tell me where to go?
I'm just floating in the wind,
Looking for a place to grow.

I needed a bit of dirt—
I found enough for me!
My roots will dig down deep.
Water and nutrients are key.

I know I need some sunlight—
What keeps blocking out the sun?
I reach high between the shadows,
But then comes another one!

Describe a habitat near your home where a dandelion seed could get all the air, sunlight, water, and nutrients it needs to grow. **Answers will vary.**

Draw a line to match each plant to the habitat where it grows.

The **oak tree** has thick bark to protect the water inside while living in a dry habitat.

Cattails have fast-growing roots to anchor them in moving water.

Seagrass has many wide leaves to absorb the sunlight in shallow water.

Predict what will happen at the end of each experiment.

Callie plants two seeds in two pots.

Then she covers one plant so it won't get any light.

Plants collect sunlight with their leaves to make food. They do that by using chlorophyll, which keeps their leaves green. Plants need sunlight to make them grow.

Draw your prediction.

Brian plants two seeds in two pots.

Then he stops watering one plant.

Plants soak up water with their roots. Then the water travels to the leaves, where it helps to make food. Plants need water to make food and to keep from drying out.

Draw your prediction.

Look for plants inside or outside your home. Where do they get the sunlight and water that they need?

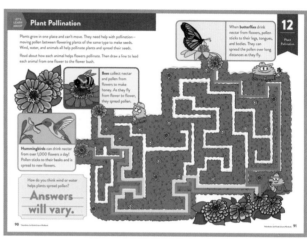

Plant Pollination

Plants grow in one place and can't move. They need help with pollination—moving pollen between flowering plants of the same type to make seeds. Wind, water, and animals all help pollinate plants and spread their seeds.

Read about how each animal helps flowers pollinate. Then draw a line to lead each animal from one flower to the flower bush.

Bees collect nectar and pollen from flowers to make honey. As they fly from flower to flower, they spread pollen.

Hummingbirds can drink nectar from over 1,000 flowers a day! Pollen sticks to their beaks and is spread to new flowers.

When **butterflies** drink nectar from flowers, pollen sticks to their legs, tongues, and bodies. They can spread the pollen over long distances as they fly.

How do you think wind or water helps spread pollen? **Answers will vary.**

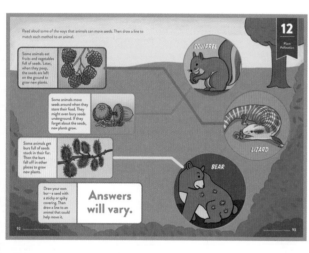

Read aloud some of the ways that animals can move seeds. Then draw a line to match each method to an animal.

Some animals eat fruits and vegetables full of seeds. Later, when they poop, the seeds are left on the ground to grow new plants.

Some animals move seeds around when they store their food. They might even bury seeds underground. If they forget about the seeds, new plants grow.

Some animals get burs full of seeds stuck in their fur. Then the burs fall off in other places to grow new plants.

Draw your own bur—a seed with a sticky or spiky covering. Then draw a line to an animal that could help move it. **Answers will vary.**

SQUIRREL · LIZARD · BEAR

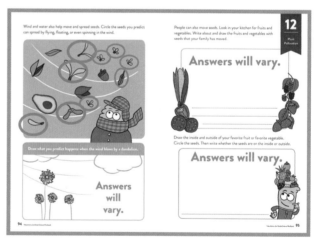

Wind and water also help move and spread seeds. Circle the seeds you predict can spread by flying, floating, or even spinning in the wind.

Draw what you predict happens when the wind blows by a dandelion. **Answers will vary.**

People can also move seeds. Look in your kitchen for fruits and vegetables. Write about and draw the fruits and vegetables with seeds that your family has moved. **Answers will vary.**

Draw the inside and outside of your favorite fruit or favorite vegetable. Circle the seeds. Then write whether the seeds are on the inside or outside. **Answers will vary.**

Engineering Design: Shoe

It's time to go to lunch, but Amelia is having trouble with one of her shoes. Why?

RESEARCH THE PROBLEM!

OBSERVE
What do you notice about the shoe? **Answers will vary.**

GATHER INFORMATION
What can you learn by touching the shoe? **Answers will vary.**

ASK QUESTIONS
What would you ask Amelia about her shoe? **Answers will vary.**

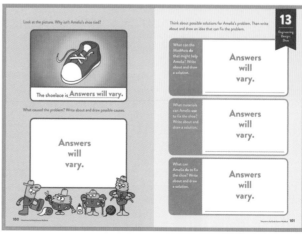

Look at the picture. Why isn't Amelia's shoe tied?

The shoelace is **Answers will vary.**

What caused the problem? Write about and draw possible causes. **Answers will vary.**

Think about possible solutions for Amelia's problem. Then write about and draw an idea that can fix the problem.

What can the MotMots do that might help Amelia? Write about and draw a solution. **Answers will vary.**

What materials can Amelia use to fix the shoe? Write about and draw a solution. **Answers will vary.**

What can Amelia do to fix the shoe? Write about and draw a solution. **Answers will vary.**

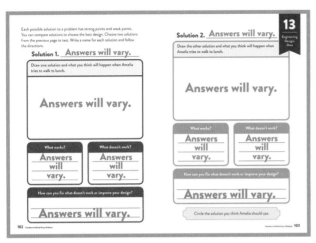

Panel (pages 102–103)

Each possible solution to a problem has strong points and weak points. You can compare solutions to choose the best design. Choose two solutions from the previous page to test. Write a name for each solution and follow the directions.

Solution 1. Answers will vary.

Draw one solution and what you think will happen when Amelia tries to walk to lunch.

Answers will vary.

What works?
Answers will vary.

What doesn't work?
Answers will vary.

How can you fix what doesn't work or improve your design?
Answers will vary.

Solution 2. Answers will vary.

Draw the other solution and what you think will happen when Amelia tries to walk to lunch.

Answers will vary.

What works?
Answers will vary.

What doesn't work?
Answers will vary.

How can you fix what doesn't work or improve your design?
Answers will vary.

Circle the solution you think Amelia should use.

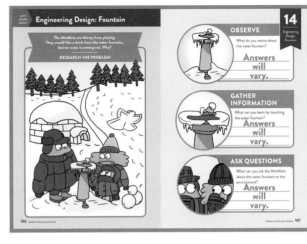

Engineering Design: Fountain

The MotMots are thirsty from playing. They would like a drink from the water fountain, but no water is coming out. Why?

RESEARCH THE PROBLEM!

OBSERVE
What do you notice about the water fountain?
Answers will vary.

GATHER INFORMATION
What can you learn by touching the water fountain?
Answers will vary.

ASK QUESTIONS
What can you ask the MotMots about the water fountain or the environment?
Answers will vary.

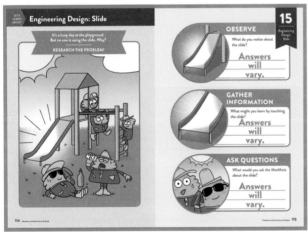

Panel (pages 108–109)

Look at the picture. Why isn't the fountain on?

The fountain is Answers will vary.

What caused the problem? Write about and draw possible causes.
Answers will vary.

Think about possible solutions for the MotMots' problem. Then write about and draw an idea that can fix the problem.

What can the MotMots do that might help? Write about and draw a solution.
Answers will vary.

What materials can the MotMots use that might help? Write about and draw a solution.
Answers will vary.

What can the MotMots bring to the park that might help? Write about and draw a solution.
Answers will vary.

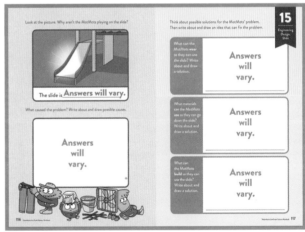

Panel (pages 110–111)

Each possible solution to a problem has strong points and weak points. You can compare solutions to choose the best design. Choose two solutions from the previous page to test. Write a name for each solution and follow the directions.

Solution 1. Answers will vary.

Draw one solution and what you think will happen the next time the MotMots press the fountain's button for a drink.

Answers will vary.

What works?
Answers will vary.

What doesn't work?
Answers will vary.

How can you fix what doesn't work or improve your design?
Answers will vary.

Solution 2. Answers will vary.

Draw the other solution and what you think will happen the next time the MotMots press the fountain's button for a drink.

Answers will vary.

What works?
Answers will vary.

What doesn't work?
Answers will vary.

How can you fix what doesn't work or improve your design?
Answers will vary.

Circle the solution you think the MotMots should use.

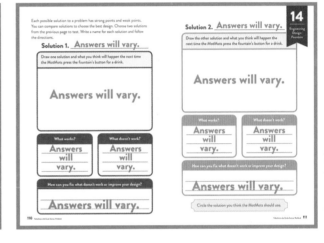

Panel (pages 114–115)

Engineering Design: Slide

It's a busy day at the playground. But no one is using the slide. Why?

RESEARCH THE PROBLEM!

OBSERVE
What do you notice about the slide?
Answers will vary.

GATHER INFORMATION
What might you learn by touching the slide?
Answers will vary.

ASK QUESTIONS
What would you ask the MotMots about the slide?
Answers will vary.

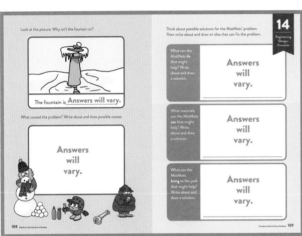

Panel (pages 116–117)

Look at the picture. Why aren't the MotMots playing on the slide?

The slide is Answers will vary.

What caused the problem? Write about and draw possible causes.
Answers will vary.

Think about possible solutions for the MotMots' problem. Then write about and draw an idea that can fix the problem.

What can the MotMots wear so they can use the slide? Write about and draw a solution.
Answers will vary.

What materials can the MotMots use so they can go down the slide? Write about and draw a solution.
Answers will vary.

What can the MotMots build so they can use the slide? Write about and draw a solution.
Answers will vary.

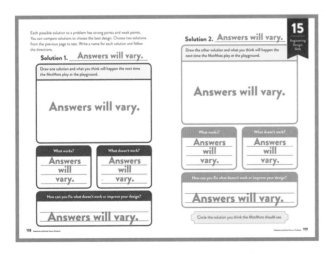

Panel (pages 118–119)

Each possible solution to a problem has strong points and weak points. You can compare solutions to choose the best design. Choose two solutions from the previous page to test. Write a name for each solution and follow the directions.

Solution 1. Answers will vary.

Draw one solution and what you think will happen the next time the MotMots play at the playground.

Answers will vary.

What works?
Answers will vary.

What doesn't work?
Answers will vary.

How can you fix what doesn't work or improve your design?
Answers will vary.

Solution 2. Answers will vary.

Draw the other solution and what you think will happen the next time the MotMots play at the playground.

Answers will vary.

What works?
Answers will vary.

What doesn't work?
Answers will vary.

How can you fix what doesn't work or improve your design?
Answers will vary.

Circle the solution you think the MotMots should use.

Odd Dot
175 Fifth Avenue
New York, NY 10010
OddDot.com

ISBN: 978-1-250-30726-2

WRITER   Megan Hewes Butler

ILLUSTRATOR   Tae Won Yu

EDUCATIONAL CONSULTANT   Lindsay Frevert

CHARACTER DESIGNER   Anna-Maria Jung

COVER ILLUSTRATOR   Anna-Maria Jung

BACK COVER ILLUSTRATION   Chad Thomas

BADGE EMBROIDERER   El Patcha

INTERIOR DESIGNER   Tae Won Yu

COVER DESIGNERS   Carolyn Bahar and Colleen AF Venable

EDITORS   Nathalie Le Du and Justin Krasner

Our books may be purchased in bulk for promotional, educational, or business use. Please contact your
local bookseller or the Macmillan Corporate and Premium Sales Department at (800) 221-7945 ext.
5442 or by email at MacmillanSpecialMarkets@macmillan.com

DISCLAIMER
The publisher and authors disclaim responsibility for any loss, injury, or damages that may result from a
reader engaging in the activities described in this book.

TinkerActive is a trademark of Odd Dot.
Printed in China by Hung Hing Off-set Printing Co. Ltd., Heshan City, Guangdong Province
First edition, 2019
10 9 8 7 6 5 4 3 2 1

For the activity on page 9

For the activity on page 17

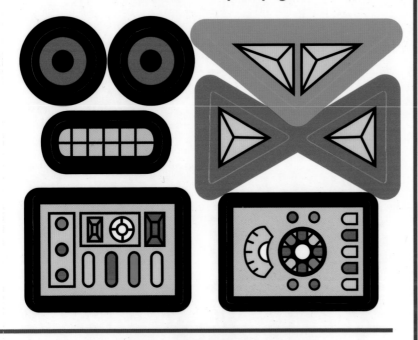

For the activity on
page 105

Sticker your *TINKERACTIVE EXPERT* poster
after you complete each project.

_____
(Your Name Here)

IS A TINKERACTIVE EXPERT!

PLACE YOUR MATH BADGE HERE!

PLACE YOUR SCIENCE BADGE HERE!

PLACE YOUR ENGLISH LANGUAGE ARTS BADGE HERE!

PROJECT 1   PROJECT 2   PROJECT 3

PROJECT 4   PROJECT 5   PROJECT 6

PROJECT 7   PROJECT 8   PROJECT 9

PROJECT 10   PROJECT 11   PROJECT 12

PROJECT 13   PROJECT 14   PROJECT 15

PROJECT 1   PROJECT 2   PROJECT 3

PROJECT 4   PROJECT 5   PROJECT 6

PROJECT 7   PROJECT 8   PROJECT 9

PROJECT 10   PROJECT 11   PROJECT 12

PROJECT 13   PROJECT 14   PROJECT 15

PROJECT 1   PROJECT 2   PROJECT 3

PROJECT 4   PROJECT 5   PROJECT 6

PROJECT 7   PROJECT 8   PROJECT 9

PROJECT 10   PROJECT 11   PROJECT 12

PROJECT 13   PROJECT 14   PROJECT 15

 COLLECT THEM ALL!